Mirrors to the Soul

Techniques for Deep Self-Reflection

Author – Stan Barren

Brought to you by InspirationDB

Legal and Copyright Disclaimer

Exclusive Offer Inside!

Have you ever found yourself questioning the direction of your life or wondering if there's more to your journey? We have something special just for you - a roadmap to finding that missing piece, a guide to uncovering the purpose that fuels your passion and drives your ambitions.

Introducing "The Ultimate Guide to Finding Your Life's Purpose."

Whether you're at a crossroads, feeling lost, or simply curious about what makes life truly meaningful, this comprehensive e-book has the insights, exercises, and stories to illuminate your path.

And here's the best part: We're giving it away for FREE! Don't miss out! Subscribe to our email newsletter now and get instant access to "The Ultimate Guide to Finding Your Life's Purpose." Discover the passion, meaning, and drive that's waiting within you.

Get now from InspirationDB.com/FREE

Table of Contents

Introduction

In the fast-paced world of today, where instant gratification often overshadows profound fulfillment, taking a pause to look within can seem like an arduous task. Yet, the journey to self-understanding, to diving deep into the intricate layers of our psyche, remains one of the most profound adventures one can embark on.

"Mirrors to the Soul: Techniques for Deep Self-Reflection" was born out of a desire to guide you on this quest of inner exploration, a voyage that has been championed by sages, philosophers, and thinkers across different cultures and epochs.

At the heart of this book is the belief that self-awareness is not just a luxury for the introspective or the philosophical, but a necessity for anyone looking to lead a fulfilling and authentic life. By truly understanding ourselves, we pave the way for genuine growth, improved relationships, and a deeper connection to the world around us.

Yet, the path to self-awareness is neither linear nor universally defined. It varies, enriched by the tapestry of global practices and traditions that have evolved over millennia.

"Mirrors to the Soul" is more than just a guide, it's an invitation. An invitation to immerse yourself in the myriad techniques from around the world, each offering a unique lens through which you can view yourself.

From the meditative traditions of the East to the analytical methodologies of the West, from indigenous rituals that connect us to the earth to modern-day technologies that leverage the digital realm for self-reflection, this book aims to be a comprehensive companion on your journey within.

Whether you're a novice at self-reflection or someone who has been on this path for a while, the techniques and insights contained within these pages promise a deeper understanding of the self. Let's embark on this journey together, diving deep, challenging our perceptions, and unveiling the true essence that lies within.

Why Self-Reflection is Important

Self-reflection is a powerful process of introspection where individuals actively engage in understanding their thoughts, emotions, decisions, and behaviors. By turning their focus inward, they seek clarity about their core values, beliefs, and aspirations. Its significance spans across multiple dimensions of our lives, both personally and professionally.

Firstly, self-awareness is the foundation for personal growth. Without a clear understanding of our own strengths, weaknesses, passions, and fears, our ability to evolve becomes limited. Self-reflection acts as a mirror, showing us our true selves, beyond the external personas we often present to the world. This genuine self-awareness is the first step toward any meaningful change in our lives.

Secondly, self-reflection enhances emotional intelligence. By regularly examining our reactions to various situations and our interactions with others, we develop a deeper understanding of our emotional triggers and patterns.

This heightened emotional awareness allows us to better manage our feelings, improving our relationships and communication with others. Emotionally intelligent individuals can empathize more easily, exhibit better patience, and resolve conflicts more amicably.

Moreover, self-reflection aids in decision-making. Every day, we are bombarded with choices, from the mundane to the life-altering. Reflecting on our past decisions, their outcomes, and our underlying motivations can equip us with better judgment for future choices. By recognizing past misjudgments or biases, we can make decisions that are more aligned with our long-term goals and core values.

Additionally, it fosters a sense of accountability and responsibility. Instead of attributing our actions and their outcomes entirely to external factors, we learn to recognize our role in the events of our lives. This empowers us to take control of our future, understanding that our decisions and actions directly influence the course of our journey.

Lastly, self-reflection is a conduit to inner peace. In an increasingly chaotic world, finding moments of stillness to simply introspect can be incredibly therapeutic. It provides a respite from external pressures, allowing us to connect with our innermost thoughts and feelings. Over time, this practice can lead to greater mental clarity, reduced stress, and a deeper sense of fulfillment.

In conclusion, self-reflection is not just a self-indulgent exercise but a critical tool for personal and professional development. It allows us to understand ourselves better, make informed decisions, build stronger relationships, and lead a life that resonates with our true essence. In embracing this practice, we not only enrich our own lives but also positively impact those around us.

Purpose of the Book

In the fast-paced world we inhabit, it's easy to get lost in the daily grind, overlooking the deeper aspects of who we are and what truly matters. This negligence often results in feelings of emptiness, disconnection, and a lack of fulfillment. "Mirrors to the Soul" has been crafted as a beacon for those wandering in such internal obscurity, aiming to illuminate the pathways leading to genuine self-understanding and authentic living.

The essence of this book is to bridge the rich tapestry of global self-reflective practices with the innate human need for introspection. Every culture, from the sprawling metropolises of the West to the serene villages of the East, has developed its unique tools for internal exploration.

By diving into these varied techniques, we embark on a journey that transcends borders, connecting us to the shared human experience of seeking self-awareness.

Moreover, the purpose isn't merely to inform but to inspire transformative action. The techniques and stories contained within these pages aren't just theoretical expositions; they are practical methods tested by time and tradition. Readers are not only introduced to these techniques but are also guided on how to integrate them into their daily lives.

Finally, in an age dominated by technology, this book also acknowledges the modern tools and scientific methodologies contributing to the self-reflective realm. As such, "Mirrors to the Soul" serves as a comprehensive guide, merging ancient wisdom with contemporary insights, all aimed at one sacred goal: to help individuals unlock their true potential by understanding their innermost selves.

What the Reader Can Expect to Gain

Insight into Self: At its core, "Mirrors to the Soul" seeks to offer readers a profound journey inward. As they navigate the pages and practices encapsulated within, they will uncover layers of their psyche previously unexplored.

The techniques showcased will help peel away facades, offering readers an unvarnished look into their desires, fears, strengths, and areas for growth. Such insights are invaluable for anyone aiming to truly understand themselves and find meaning in their life's narrative.

Diverse Techniques: The book presents a rich tapestry of self-reflective techniques stemming from diverse corners of the world. From the meditative depths of Eastern philosophies to the empirical rigors of Western psychology, readers will gain exposure to a wide spectrum of tools.

This ensures that each individual, regardless of background or predisposition, will find techniques that resonate with them, granting them flexibility and choice in their self-reflective journey.

Cultural Appreciation: Beyond personal development, readers will embark on a cultural voyage, understanding how civilizations across epochs have approached the idea of self-reflection. This exploration underscores the universality of introspection, helping readers appreciate the interconnectedness of human thought and the shared pursuit of inner understanding.

Practical Applications: This isn't a book of mere theory. Emphasis has been placed on the actionable. As readers progress, they will find tangible exercises, guided sessions, and practical advice that can be seamlessly integrated into their daily lives.

Whether it's through journal prompts or detailed steps to harness modern technological tools, readers will be equipped to make self-reflection an ongoing practice.

Enhanced Well-being: Delving deep into oneself and confronting truths can be transformative. As readers apply the techniques learned, they can expect improvements in mental and emotional well-being. A clearer understanding of oneself often leads to better decision-making, improved relationships, and an overarching sense of contentment and peace.

Community and Connection: Embedded within the book are tales, anecdotes, and case studies of individuals who've traversed the path of self-reflection.

These stories serve not just as inspiration but also as testament to a shared human experience. Readers will find solace in knowing they're not alone in their introspective journey and might even be compelled to share their own stories, fostering a sense of community and connection.

Brief overview of techniques covered from different cultures

The tapestry of human history is interwoven with diverse philosophies and practices cantered on self-awareness and self-reflection. From the contemplative traditions of the East to the ritualistic practices of indigenous tribes, myriad techniques have emerged that aid individuals in diving deep into their psyche.

In the Western world, the art of journaling has become an introspective tool, a quiet conversation between the self and the written word, allowing for self-exploration and emotional processing. Psychotherapy, with its roots in European psychology, provides a structured dialogue between a therapist and an individual, unearthing patterns, traumas, and insights.

In contrast, the East, with its ancient wisdom, offers practices like mindfulness, rooted in Buddhist traditions, emphasizing the power of the present moment. The practice of Self-Inquiry, or 'Atma Vichara' in Hinduism, nudges one towards understanding their true nature beyond the physical and the ephemeral. Daoism from China, through the principle of Wu Wei, accentuates the idea of 'non-doing' or 'non-action' as a pathway to alignment with the natural flow of life.

Venturing further, indigenous practices worldwide encapsulate the essence of man's connection to nature and self. Native American tribes have long held sweat lodge ceremonies, where intense heat and traditional chanting lead participants towards visions and deep self-reflection.

In Africa, the philosophy of Ubuntu underlines interconnectedness, proposing that our sense of self is intrinsically linked to our community. The Aboriginal Dreamtime stories of Australia aren't just tales; they are spiritual journeys, guiding listeners into the inner recesses of their minds and the vastness of the universe.

In our modern era, a fusion of ancient wisdom and new-age science has given rise to techniques grounded in neurology and cognitive sciences. Neuro-Linguistic Programming (NLP) seeks to reframe and reprogram the mind's language, while Cognitive Behavioral Therapy (CBT) emphasizes recognizing and restructuring harmful patterns of thought.

Art and creativity, transcending cultural boundaries, have always been mirrors to the soul. From the rhythm-infused dances of tribal Africa to the serene brush strokes in Japanese Zen painting, artistic expression has been a gateway to understanding one's emotions, desires, and fears.

In essence, each culture, with its unique heritage and understanding of the world, has contributed invaluable tools to humanity's collective repository of self-reflective practices. Adopting and adapting these techniques in our individual quests can provide fresh perspectives and profound insights.

Chapter 1: The Importance of Self-Awareness

In our fast-paced world, rife with distractions and external pressures, there's a quiet power that few fully harness: self-awareness. This chapter delves into the fundamental essence of self-awareness, seeking to unearth its significance in our lives.

At its core, self-awareness is the conscious knowledge of one's own character, feelings, desires, and motivations. It's akin to holding a mirror up to our souls, seeing our authentic selves reflected back, flaws and all. Yet, while some may argue that introspection is an indulgence, or even a luxury in today's world, the true depth of its importance goes far beyond mere self-contemplation.

The journey to understand oneself better is as old as humanity itself. Philosophers, from Socrates with his injunction, "Know thyself," to modern thinkers, have emphasized the value of understanding oneself. Why? Because knowing oneself is the first step in making intentional, meaningful choices in life. It's the foundation upon which emotional intelligence is built, fostering improved relationships, stronger decision-making skills, and a sense of purpose.

This chapter aims to explore the multifaceted benefits of self-awareness, its pivotal role in personal development, and its intrinsic value in cultivating a fulfilled life. Through understanding the importance of self-awareness, readers will be better equipped to appreciate the techniques and practices detailed in the subsequent chapters, seeing them not just as tools, but as keys to unlocking a more profound understanding of the self.

Definitions: Self-Awareness, Self-Reflection

Self-Awareness

Self-awareness is a multifaceted cognitive ability that enables individuals to recognize, understand, and be conscious of their own thoughts, feelings, behaviors, beliefs, and motivations. It acts as an internal mirror, allowing one to see themselves from a third-person perspective, providing insights into one's emotional state, desires, strengths, weaknesses, and potential triggers.

Having self-awareness means that a person can comprehend how they are perceived by others and how their own actions and feelings might influence or be influenced by external factors.

A significant component of emotional intelligence, self-awareness is pivotal for interpersonal interactions and personal growth. Individuals with high self-awareness tend to have a better grasp of their own emotions and can more efficiently navigate challenging situations without succumbing to impulsive reactions.

This awareness doesn't always imply that one has to agree with external perceptions, but rather that they are conscious of them and can choose how to act on them. Cultivating self-awareness often involves introspective practices and can be enhanced through activities such as journaling, meditation, and feedback from trusted peers or mentors.

Self-Reflection

Closely linked to self-awareness, self-reflection is an active and intentional process of thinking deeply about one's experiences, actions, feelings, and responses.

While self-awareness is the conscious recognition of one's inner state and attributes, self-reflection dives deeper into analysing, questioning, and evaluating those states and behaviors. It's akin to conducting an internal audit of one's mind and soul, aiming to understand past choices, learn from experiences, and make informed decisions for the future.

Self-reflection is essential for personal growth and self-improvement, as it encourages individuals to confront their biases, acknowledge their mistakes, and identify areas for development. The process can sometimes be challenging, as it may uncover uncomfortable truths or memories, but confronting these aspects is crucial for genuine personal evolution.

Techniques for fostering self-reflection include deep meditation, journaling, engaging in thought-provoking conversations, and setting aside quiet moments regularly to ponder one's thoughts and actions. When practiced consistently, self-reflection can lead to profound insights, clearer decision-making, and a deeper connection with one's core values and beliefs.

The Psychology behind Self-awareness

The Foundations of Self-Awareness in Cognitive Psychology:

At its core, self-awareness emerges from cognitive processes. Cognitive psychology, which studies mental functions like memory, problem-solving, and thinking, acknowledges self-awareness as a higher-order cognitive function.

This essentially means that self-awareness isn't merely recognizing oneself in a mirror but understanding oneself within a broader context. It's the realization that one can have thoughts about one's thoughts, feelings about one's feelings, and beliefs about one's beliefs.

This metacognitive ability to "think about one's thinking" sets humans apart from many other species. Through introspection, individuals can evaluate their internal states, helping them understand their strengths, weaknesses, emotions, beliefs, and motivations.

Developmental Origins of Self-Awareness:

From a developmental perspective, self-awareness doesn't emerge instantly. Instead, it's a gradual process, most evident in the growth stages of children. Infants, for instance, don't start with a conscious recognition of themselves.

It's only around the age of 18 to 24 months that most toddlers begin to exhibit signs of self-recognition, a milestone often tested using the "mirror test." As children grow, their self-awareness evolves, progressing from basic self-recognition to the understanding that they have a private inner world, distinct from others.

By the time they reach adolescence, a period characterized by intense identity exploration, their self-awareness becomes more sophisticated, enabling deeper introspection and a heightened sense of individuality.

The Social Context of Self-Awareness:

Social psychology offers another dimension, emphasizing the role of interpersonal relationships and societal structures in shaping self-awareness.

In essence, our self-concept often mirrors how we believe others perceive us. This is encapsulated in Charles Horton Cooley's concept of the "looking-glass self," where our self-view is shaped through the "mirror" of social interaction.

Further, the theory of social comparison, proposed by Leon Festinger, suggests that people determine their worth and identity by comparing themselves to others, particularly when there's a lack of objective means to evaluate certain aspects of themselves.

Through such comparisons, individuals can develop a clearer sense of self-awareness, understanding where they fit within a social context.

The Therapeutic Value in Understanding Self-Awareness:

Within the realm of clinical psychology, self-awareness is a cornerstone of many therapeutic practices. Psychologists and therapists often emphasize the importance of enhancing self-awareness in their patients, believing that understanding oneself better can lead to improved mental health, better decision-making, and increased emotional intelligence.

Techniques such as mindfulness meditation, journaling, and cognitive-behavioral therapies are often employed to foster and develop this understanding.

It's posited that by increasing self-awareness, individuals can better identify negative patterns, make proactive changes, and cultivate a life that aligns more closely with their true selves and values.

In sum, self-awareness is multifaceted, intertwined with various domains of psychology. Its relevance stretches from the individual's internal cognitive processes to broader societal interactions, highlighting its significance in both personal and interpersonal domains of human life.

Why Self-Awareness is Crucial for Personal Development

Self-awareness, often heralded as the cornerstone of personal development, is the conscious knowledge and recognition of one's character, feelings, motives, and desires. This introspective capability allows individuals to analyze and understand their thoughts, emotions, and behaviors, ensuring that they remain in alignment with their core values and beliefs. But why is this inner understanding so essential for personal growth?

Facilitation of Change: The first step towards meaningful change is recognizing the need for it. Without self-awareness, individuals might drift through life unaware of self-limiting beliefs, negative patterns of thinking, or behaviors that hinder progress. By being in tune with oneself, one can identify areas of improvement and take actionable steps towards personal and professional growth.

Better Decision Making: Self-aware individuals tend to have a deeper understanding of what they truly want and what aligns with their core beliefs. This clarity plays a crucial role in making decisions that are conducive to one's long-term happiness and success. Whether it's career choices, personal relationships, or day-to-day decisions, a heightened sense of self-awareness equips individuals to navigate life's crossroads with confidence and conviction.

Emotional Regulation: Recognizing one's emotions, understanding the triggers, and knowing how best to manage them is a benefit of self-awareness. Emotional intelligence, a by-product of this understanding, enables individuals to handle stress, confrontations, and emotional challenges with a level-headedness that can be invaluable in personal and professional settings.

Improved Relationships: By understanding oneself, an individual can better understand others. Self-aware individuals are often more empathetic, understanding, and better communicators. They can discern their own emotions and reactions and how these can affect interpersonal dynamics. This recognition helps in fostering healthier and more harmonious relationships.

Setting and Achieving Goals: Personal development is closely linked with goal-setting and achievement. Self-aware individuals, having a clearer understanding of their strengths, weaknesses, passions, and aspirations, can set more realistic and aligned goals. Their insight into their own motivations can serve as a driving force, propelling them towards the accomplishment of these objectives.

Enhanced Resilience: Life is replete with challenges and setbacks. Self-aware individuals have the advantage of understanding their coping mechanisms, strengths, and areas of vulnerability. This knowledge allows them to navigate challenges with a resilient mindset, learning from failures and bouncing back more efficiently.

In essence, self-awareness is the foundation upon which personal development is built. It offers a mirror to one's soul, reflecting both strengths to be harnessed and areas to be developed. By continuously engaging in introspection and seeking self-awareness, individuals not only enrich their own lives but also contribute positively to the world around them, making it an indispensable tool in the journey of personal growth.

Chapter 2: Western Approaches to Self-Reflection

The Western world, with its rich tapestry of philosophical, psychological, and cultural advancements, has long grappled with the concept of self and the art of introspection. Rooted in ancient Greco-Roman traditions, the adage "Know Thyself" chiseled on the Temple of Apollo at Delphi, serves as a testament to the emphasis placed on personal understanding and self-awareness thousands of years ago.

In this chapter, we will embark on a journey through the Western approaches to self-reflection. We will uncover how the act of introspection has been shaped and refined over the centuries, manifesting in various forms from structured psychotherapy to the journals that many keep by their bedside.

Specifically, we'll delve deep into three prominent Western methods: Journaling, with its narrative power to mold our life's stories; Psychotherapy and Counselling, offering structured environments for individuals to untangle their thoughts with professional guidance; and Mindfulness and Meditation, practices that, while having Eastern origins, have been widely adapted and secularized to fit the Western paradigm.

The Western landscape of introspection, vast and varied, offers myriad tools and techniques. Each, in its unique way, serves as a mirror to the soul, allowing us to view ourselves more clearly, understanding our motivations, desires, fears, and dreams. As we progress, you'll gain insights into how you might weave these practices into your own journey of self-discovery.

Stan Barren

Journaling: A Deep Dive into the Art and Science of Self-Expression

Introduction to Journaling:

Journaling, at its core, is the practice of recording thoughts, feelings, observations, and experiences in a structured or unstructured manner. This age-old technique has been utilized by countless individuals throughout history, from renowned writers and thinkers to everyday people seeking clarity and self-understanding.

Its appeal lies in its simplicity: all one requires is a pen and paper (or its digital equivalent) and a few quiet moments of reflection.

Historical Context:

The act of keeping a journal dates back centuries, with some of the earliest known diaries being attributed to ancient Roman and Asian civilizations. These writings, often preserved on scrolls or bound pages, served as a testament to the writer's personal history, societal observations, and innermost contemplations.

Over time, figures like Anne Frank, Samuel Pepys, and Virginia Woolf have left indelible marks in the world of literature and history through their intimate journal entries.

Therapeutic Benefits:

Journaling is more than just a record-keeping activity; it's a therapeutic tool. Numerous studies have highlighted the positive psychological impacts of journaling. Regularly penning down thoughts can lead to better mental clarity, improved problem-solving abilities, and enhanced emotional well-being.

The act of transferring thoughts from mind to paper can provide an emotional release, acting as a form of catharsis. Additionally, reflecting upon written entries can offer insights into behavioral patterns, enabling individuals to identify and address potential areas of personal growth.

Types of Journaling:

The beauty of journaling lies in its adaptability. There are various forms and styles, each catering to different needs and purposes:

Gratitude Journal: Focusing on the positive, this form of journaling helps individuals recognize and appreciate the good in their lives, fostering a more optimistic mindset.

Dream Journal: Used to document and interpret dreams, aiding in the understanding of subconscious thoughts and feelings.

Travel Journal: A chronicle of one's journeys, capturing experiences, sights, and learnings from different cultures.

Bullet Journal: A combination of to-do lists, schedules, and reflections, aimed at improving productivity and organization.

Art Journal: Incorporating drawings, paintings, and other forms of visual art alongside or in lieu of written entries.

Digital Journaling:

The digital age has brought with it a new wave of journaling. Many now prefer to use apps or online platforms, citing advantages like portability, multimedia integration (photos, videos, audio clips), and enhanced security with password protections.

While purists might argue in favor of the tactile feel of pen on paper, digital journals cater to a generation accustomed to screens, offering a blend of traditional introspection with modern convenience.

In Conclusion:

Journaling stands as a testament to the human need for expression and introspection. Whether scribbled in an age-worn notebook or typed into a sleek app, the act remains a powerful tool for self-discovery, reflection, and personal growth. As with any practice, its true benefits are realized through consistency, sincerity, and a genuine willingness to engage with one's inner world.

Psychotherapy and Counselling

Psychotherapy

Psychotherapy, often colloquially referred to as "talk therapy," is a broad term used to describe a range of treatments that address emotional challenges and certain mental disorders. It offers a safe, confidential environment where individuals can discuss their feelings, thoughts, and behaviors with a trained professional. The ultimate goal of psychotherapy is to help individuals lead happier, more functional, and fulfilling lives.

There are different types of psychotherapy, each with its methods and techniques. For instance, cognitive-behavioral therapy (CBT) focuses on identifying and challenging negative thought patterns and behaviors.

On the other hand, psychoanalysis, founded by Sigmund Freud, delves deep into the unconscious mind, examining early childhood experiences to understand current behaviors. Another method, humanistic therapy, emphasizes personal growth and self-fulfillment.

The length and frequency of psychotherapy sessions can vary widely, depending on the individual's needs and the nature of the problem. While some might benefit from just a few sessions, others might attend regular sessions for months or even years. Regardless of its duration or type, a successful psychotherapy experience hinges on developing a trusting, open relationship between the therapist and the patient.

Counselling

Counselling is a therapeutic process aimed at assisting individuals in managing or overcoming personal, social, or psychological challenges.

While there's a significant overlap between counselling and psychotherapy, counselling often focuses on specific issues for a defined period. It provides individuals with tools and strategies to cope with immediate concerns, be it marital difficulties, stress management, or career decision-making.

Counsellors adopt a holistic approach, often examining the emotional, mental, and social well-being of their clients. They work in various settings, such as schools, rehabilitation centers, hospitals, or private practices.

Just like psychotherapists, counsellors are also trained to employ different techniques tailored to their client's unique needs. For instance, career counsellors use aptitude and vocational tests to advise clients on career choices, while marriage and family therapists might use systems theory to understand family dynamics.

One primary distinction between counselling and psychotherapy lies in the depth and duration. Counselling often deals with present-day concerns and is typically more short-term and goal-oriented. In contrast, psychotherapy may delve deeper into long-standing psychological patterns and can be more extended.

Both psychotherapy and counselling can be invaluable tools for individuals facing mental health challenges or life's adversities. The choice between the two usually depends on the nature and depth of the issues at hand, as well as personal preferences.

Mindfulness and Meditation

Mindfulness

Mindfulness is the practice of being fully present in the moment, aware of your surroundings, and not overly reactive or overwhelmed by what's happening around you.

Stemming from ancient Buddhist teachings, mindfulness has gained immense popularity in the West in recent decades, especially in the context of reducing stress and improving mental well-being.

At its core, mindfulness encourages a kind and non-judgmental attention to your thoughts, feelings, and sensory experiences in the current moment.

By doing so, one can break the habitual cycle of getting lost in thoughts, which often revolve around past regrets or future anxieties.

It's a practice that doesn't seek to eliminate thinking but to offer a space to observe thoughts without getting caught up in their narrative.

Mindfulness can be cultivated through various means. One of the most common is through mindfulness meditation. However, the practice can also be applied to daily activities such as eating, walking, or even doing household chores.

The idea is to fully engage with the present activity without letting the mind wander aimlessly.

The benefits of mindfulness are backed by numerous scientific studies. Regular practice has been linked to reduced levels of stress, anxiety, and depression.

It has also been found to improve concentration, increase emotional resilience, and even boost immune system function.

Meditation

Meditation, in its broadest sense, is a practice where an individual uses a technique, such as focusing the mind on a particular object, thought, or activity, to train attention and awareness, and achieve a mentally clear and emotionally calm and stable state.

It has been practiced since antiquity in numerous religious traditions and beliefs. There are many types of meditation techniques, each with its objectives and methods. Some of the most well-known include:

Concentration Meditation: This involves focusing on a single point, which could be following the breath, repeating a single word or mantra, staring at a candle flame, or listening to a repetitive gong. If the practitioner's mind wanders, they simply have to bring it back to the chosen point of focus.

Loving-kindness Meditation (Metta): The aim here is to cultivate an attitude of love and kindness towards everything, even an individual's adversaries or sources of stress.

Body Scan or Progressive Relaxation: This encourages individuals to scan their bodies for areas of tension, promoting relaxation and calmness.

Mindfulness Meditation: Stemming from Buddhist traditions, this encourages practitioners to observe wandering thoughts as they drift through the mind. The intention isn't to judge the thoughts or get involved but to be aware of each note as it arises.

Guided Meditation: This type, also known as guided imagery, involves imagining a peaceful and calming scene guided by a teacher or recording.

Meditation's benefits span from mental and emotional to physiological. Regular practitioners often report reduced anxiety, sharper concentration, better emotional well-being, and improved sleep.

From a physiological standpoint, meditation has been shown to lower blood pressure, enhance the immune system, and even alter the brain's structure and function, resulting in increased capacity for memory, empathy, and resilience.

Together, mindfulness and meditation form a harmonious duo, promoting a state of inner peace, clarity, and grounded-ness in the present moment. By integrating these practices into daily life, individuals can navigate the complexities of modern life with greater ease and equanimity.

Chapter 3: Eastern Philosophies and Self-Reflection

In the ever-bustling and dynamic landscapes of Eastern cultures, there lies a deep reservoir of ancient wisdom that emphasizes the importance of introspection and self-awareness.

From the snow-capped Himalayas to the serene temples of Kyoto, Eastern philosophies have, for millennia, provided pathways for individuals to connect with their innermost selves, offering a counterbalance to the external chaos of the world. These teachings, though originating from diverse traditions, hold a common thread, understanding the self as a means to achieve harmony with the universe.

This chapter will journey across three significant pillars of Eastern thought, Buddhism, Hinduism, and Daoism. Each, in its unique way, offers techniques and insights into the process of self-reflection. Whether it's the practice of mindfulness rooted in Buddhist teachings, the profound self-inquiry of Hindu philosophy, or the embracing of 'non-doing' from Daoist traditions, these ancient systems provide tools for deep introspection that are remarkably relevant, even in our modern times.

In embracing the teachings of the East, we are not only exploring methodologies or techniques but are also opening ourselves to a world of stories, parables, and philosophies that transcend time. They invite us to dive deep, challenging our current perceptions and encouraging transformative realizations. As we peel back the layers of these profound traditions, readers are encouraged to approach with an open heart, allowing these age-old wisdoms to resonate, reflect, and perhaps, redefine their understanding of self.

Buddhism and Mindfulness

Buddhism is a spiritual tradition and philosophy that originated in India over 2,500 years ago during the time of Siddhartha Gautama, who later became known as the Buddha, or "the awakened one." Central to Buddhism is the understanding of the impermanent nature of reality and the inherent suffering that comes with human existence. This suffering (often referred to as "dukkha") is attributed to our attachments, desires, and ignorance.

The Four Noble Truths form the foundation of Buddhist teaching. They diagnose human suffering, its cause, its cessation, and the path leading to its cessation. The path, called the Noble Eightfold Path, provides ethical and mental guidelines intended to lead its practitioners away from suffering and towards enlightenment and Nirvana – a state of ultimate liberation from the cycle of birth, death, and rebirth.

Mindfulness in Buddhism

Mindfulness, known as "sati" in Pali and "smṛti" in Sanskrit, is a key practice in the Buddhist tradition. It means "to remember" or "to keep in mind," and it refers to the cultivation of a specific kind of attentive awareness to one's thoughts, emotions, and actions, as well as to the world around.

Mindfulness is an integral part of the Noble Eightfold Path, specifically under "Right Mindfulness." It involves intentionally focusing one's attention on the present moment and accepting it without any judgment. This form of meditation is practiced not just during formal sitting sessions but can also be integrated into everyday activities, such as walking, eating, or even speaking.

Buddhist mindfulness practices emphasize observing the Four Foundations of Mindfulness:

Mindfulness of the Body (kāyānupassanā): This involves being deeply aware of the physical body and its sensations, including practices like body scans and mindful walking.

Mindfulness of Feelings or Sensations (vedanānupassanā): This is about observing feelings in their varying forms – pleasant, unpleasant, or neutral, and understanding their impermanent nature.

Mindfulness of Mind or Consciousness (cittānupassanā): This focuses on observing the mind's state and qualities, such as concentration, distraction, anger, or joy.

Mindfulness of Dhammas (principles or teachings): This involves observing how certain phenomena, like the Five Hindrances or the Seven Factors of Enlightenment, are present or absent in one's experience.

Mindfulness, as derived from Buddhist practices, has been integrated into many contemporary therapeutic methodologies due to its efficacy in promoting mental well-being. Jon Kabat-Zinn, for instance, developed the Mindfulness-Based Stress Reduction (MBSR) program, which has been instrumental in introducing mindfulness to the West in a secular context, showing benefits for various psychological and physical ailments. While the modern versions of mindfulness can be separated from their Buddhist origins, the principles remain similar, emphasizing awareness, presence, and acceptance.

Hinduism and Self-Inquiry

Hinduism: One of the world's oldest religions, Hinduism offers a rich tapestry of teachings, scriptures, and practices that revolve around the nature of existence, the self, and the ultimate reality.

It doesn't have a single founder, religious text, or institutional structure, making it unique and diverse. At its core, Hinduism emphasizes the interconnection of all beings and the underlying universal spirit, often referred to as Brahman.

The idea of the 'self' or 'soul' in Hinduism is often denoted by the Sanskrit term 'Atman.' This Atman is considered the true self, unchanging, and eternal, lying beneath our transient emotions, thoughts, and physicality.

The ultimate goal in many Hindu philosophies is to realize the Atman's unity with Brahman, the supreme cosmic power or universal spirit.

Self-Inquiry (Atma-Vichara): Self-inquiry, known as "Atma-Vichara" in Sanskrit, is a potent meditative practice rooted in the Hindu tradition. Its main objective is to understand and realize one's true nature or self. This method was popularized in modern times by the Indian sage Ramana Maharshi, although it can trace its origins back to ancient Hindu scriptures, particularly the Upanishads.

Atma-Vichara involves introspective questioning, primarily focusing on the question "Who am I?" The aim isn't to find a verbal or conceptual answer, but to direct the mind's attention inward, towards its source.

By continuously questioning the nature of one's thoughts, emotions, and the very sense of "I", a practitioner peels away layers of false identification, ultimately revealing the Atman underneath.

To many, this practice might seem simplistic or even repetitive. However, its depth is realized when one dedicates oneself to it earnestly. The repeated contemplation of "Who am I?" challenges and eventually dissolves the ego's boundaries, leading to moments of profound insight and, ultimately, self-realization or enlightenment.

It's essential to note that while self-inquiry is a central practice in certain Hindu philosophies, Hinduism as a whole comprises a vast range of beliefs, practices, and rituals.

Different schools and sects within Hinduism might emphasize other paths (like devotion, duty, or knowledge) as means to achieve self-realization or moksha, which is liberation from the cycle of birth and death.

Daoism and Wu Wei (The concept of 'Non-doing')

Daoism (Taoism)

Daoism, often spelled as Taoism, is an ancient Chinese philosophical and spiritual tradition that emphasizes living harmoniously with the Dao, which can be loosely translated as "the Way" or "the Path." The Dao is described as the ultimate and unchanging principle that is the source of all existence, a force that flows through all life forms and governs the universe.

Daoism's foundational text, the "Tao Te Ching," attributed to Laozi (or Lao Tzu), expounds on the nature of the Dao and how one can align with it. Unlike some other philosophical or religious systems, Daoism doesn't advocate for a structured set of moral codes but instead suggests a way of being in tune with the natural order of things.

Central to Daoism is the idea of living in harmony with nature, recognizing the balance of opposites (Yin and Yang), and embracing simplicity and spontaneity in life. The interplay of Yin and Yang, the dual forces or energies in the universe, is a recurrent theme. They represent opposite qualities – light and dark, male and female, active and passive – yet they are interconnected and interdependent. For Daoist's, understanding this interdependence and balancing these energies is key to harmonious living.

Wu Wei (The concept of 'Non-doing')

Wu Wei is one of Daoism's most essential and profound concepts, and it can be challenging to grasp due to its multifaceted nature. Translated literally, "Wu Wei" means "non-doing" or "non-action."

However, it doesn't advocate for idleness or avoidance of responsibility. Instead, Wu Wei is about aligning with the natural flow of events – to act without forcing or against the grain of the universe's natural order. It's about understanding when to act and when to refrain, ensuring that actions are effortless and in harmony with the Dao.

An apt analogy for Wu Wei can be found in water's nature, often referenced in Daoist texts. Water flows naturally, seeking the path of least resistance, yet it's powerful enough to erode rock and carve valleys. Like water, someone practicing Wu Wei does not force their way but instead understands the situation's nuances and responds effortlessly and effectively.

In practical terms, Wu Wei can be seen as a state of being where actions arise from a sense of spontaneity and intuition rather than rigid planning or forceful effort. It's akin to "being in the zone" or "flow" in modern psychology, where an individual is fully immersed in an activity with a deep sense of focus and engagement.

By embracing Wu Wei, Daoist's believe one can achieve true harmony with the world, resulting in peace, balance, and effective outcomes.

In summary, Daoism, with its principle of Wu Wei, offers profound insights into harmonious living. While these concepts originated in ancient China, they hold timeless wisdom that resonates with people worldwide, advocating for balance, simplicity, and alignment with the universe's natural rhythms.

Stan Barren

Chapter 4: Indigenous Practices

In the quest for self-awareness and reflection, we often turn to well-trodden paths, those shaped by popular psychology, contemporary self-help gurus, or ancient Eastern philosophies.

Yet, beneath the canopy of our modern lives, there lies a rich tapestry of indigenous practices that have been nurtured by native tribes and communities across the globe.

These practices, often passed down through countless generations, are deeply rooted in the rhythms of nature, the wisdom of ancestors, and a profound connection to the land and its spirits.

Indigenous communities, from the Native American tribes of North America to the Aboriginal clans of Australia, have always placed a premium on understanding oneself in relation to the larger cosmos.

Their rituals, ceremonies, and storytelling traditions aren't just about connecting with each other; they serve as mirrors, reflecting an individual's place in the grand tapestry of existence.

Through dances under moonlit skies, tales whispered by firesides, and ceremonies that blend the boundaries between the earthly and the spiritual, these communities engage in profound acts of introspection and self-discovery.

This chapter delves into the heart of these indigenous practices, seeking to understand their origins, their significance, and the ways in which they foster deep self-reflection. While some of these rituals might seem distant or exotic to the contemporary reader, their essence touches on universal truths and desires.

By understanding and appreciating these practices, we not only honor the wisdom of indigenous communities but also discover new avenues for our own journey of self-exploration.

Join us as we embark on a journey through time and space, uncovering ancient practices that have stood the test of time, offering solace, understanding, and clarity to those who seek to know themselves better.

Native American Sweat Lodge Ceremonies

The Native American Sweat Lodge Ceremony is an ancient and sacred ritual practiced by numerous Indigenous tribes across North America for centuries. Often referred to simply as "sweats," these ceremonies serve as both physical and spiritual purification rites.

Structure and Materials:

At the heart of the ceremony is the sweat lodge itself, often called an "iniipi" in the Lakota language. The lodge is typically a dome-shaped structure, constructed using flexible saplings, which are bent and then covered with animal hides or, in more recent times, blankets and tarps.

The size of a sweat lodge can vary, but it's often just large enough for participants to sit in a circle. The structure is intentionally designed to be low to the ground, encouraging humility as participants must bow to enter.

Inside the lodge, there is a pit dug into the center of the earth floor where stones, heated in an exterior fire, are placed. These stones, referred to as "Grandfathers" or "Grandmother Stones" in some traditions, are central to the ceremony.

The Ceremony:

The Sweat Lodge Ceremony is a structured ritual with specific stages and prayers. Once the stones are sufficiently heated, they're brought into the lodge one at a time, using antlers or other tools. Water is then poured onto the hot stones, producing steam and raising the temperature inside the lodge.

As the lodge fills with steam, it simulates the conditions inside the womb of Mother Earth, symbolizing a return to a primal, pure state. The darkness inside further amplifies the sense of being in another world, away from everyday life.

Songs, chants, drums, and prayers punctuate the ceremony. These elements, combined with the intense heat, facilitate deep meditation, introspection, and spiritual communion. Participants often pray for healing, guidance, or give thanks. They also might seek visions or insights about challenges they're facing.

Significance and Healing:

For many Native American tribes, the sweat lodge ceremony is a means of purification, a way to cleanse the body, mind, and spirit of impurities. It's also a place to pray and connect deeply with the Creator and ancestral spirits. The intense physical conditions – the heat, the steam, the darkness – serve to break down barriers and foster a sense of unity among participants.

The sweat also offers therapeutic benefits. The heat and steam can promote detoxification through sweating, similar to a sauna. Moreover, the ceremonial aspect, the communal experience of sharing stories, prayers, and songs, can offer emotional and psychological healing.

Respect and Cultural Appropriation:

While the Sweat Lodge Ceremony is a cherished tradition among Native American tribes, it's essential to approach it with respect and understanding. There have been instances of non-Native individuals misappropriating or commodifying the ceremony without proper understanding, sometimes even resulting in tragic consequences. Genuine sweat lodge ceremonies are led by experienced and knowledgeable elders or spiritual leaders who understand the deep cultural and spiritual significance of the ritual.

African Ubuntu Philosophy

Introduction to Ubuntu Philosophy

The term "Ubuntu" is a Nguni Bantu term often translated as "I am because we are," reflecting a shared sense of humanity and community.

It highlights the belief that we are all bound together in ways that are both visible and invisible. It's not merely a philosophical concept but also a way of life in many African societies, guiding social interactions, decisions, and relationships.

Historical and Cultural Context

Ubuntu is deeply rooted in African ancestral wisdom and has been passed down through generations. While it's a predominant part of many Southern African cultures, its essence can be found in various African societies.

It's a guiding philosophy that predates colonization and has played a significant role in post-colonial African leadership and reconciliation processes, notably in South Africa's transition from apartheid. The Truth and Reconciliation Commission, led by Archbishop Desmond Tutu, leaned heavily on the principles of Ubuntu, emphasizing forgiveness, restoration, and community over retribution.

Principles and Beliefs

At its core, Ubuntu asserts that our humanity is mutually dependent. It's the recognition that our well-being, happiness, and misery are deeply tied to those of others. This interconnectedness means that if one person suffers, everyone suffers, and if one person thrives, the community thrives.

It teaches that attributes like kindness, compassion, tolerance, and mutual respect arise from understanding our deep interconnectedness.

Modern Implications and Applications

In today's globalized world, where individualism is often celebrated, Ubuntu offers a refreshing perspective on community and shared responsibility. It reminds us of the importance of community support, understanding, and mutual respect.

Modern organizations, especially those in Africa, have drawn from Ubuntu's principles to create collaborative and harmonious work environments. It also has implications in conflict resolution, where the focus is on healing and restoring broken relationships rather than punitive measures.

Conclusion

Ubuntu, with its emphasis on collective humanity, offers timeless wisdom. In a world grappling with divisiveness, it serves as a reminder that our shared humanity is more significant than our differences. It's a call to recognize and honor our mutual dependencies, celebrating community, compassion, and interconnectedness.

Australian Aboriginal Dreamtime Stories

A Cultural Keystone

At the heart of Australian Aboriginal spirituality and cultural identity lie the Dreamtime stories. These are the ancient narratives of the Aboriginal people and have been passed down through countless generations, connecting the present to the distant past.

Often rich with allegorical meaning, these tales serve multiple purposes: they provide entertainment, enforce moral lessons, and anchor the spiritual beliefs and practices of the Indigenous communities.

Nature and Creation

Dreamtime stories often center around the creation and the natural world. These narratives describe how ancestral spirits moved across the barren land, creating rivers, mountains, forests, and deserts.

These spirits also gave life to plants and animals, imbuing the Australian landscape with life and energy. Notable among these stories is the tale of the Rainbow Serpent, a powerful figure who shaped the landscape, created humanity, and laid down the laws for social behavior.

Morality and Lessons

These tales are not just about the world's creation and its features. Many Dreamtime stories are allegories that convey moral lessons.

They discuss the consequences of greed, the importance of sharing, the value of courage, and many other life lessons. Through these tales, younger generations learn the codes of behavior, ethics, and values that are central to Aboriginal culture.

Connections to the Land

The Dreamtime stories also emphasize the profound connection between the Aboriginal people and the land. Every mountain, river, rock, or waterhole has its own story, its own spirit, and its own life.

This interconnection underscores the Aboriginal belief in their role as the land's custodians. It is their duty to protect and preserve the land, ensuring that the spirit of the Dreamtime remains vibrant and alive.

Preservation and Continuity

Traditionally, these stories weren't written down. Instead, they were passed orally from one generation to the next. Elders, recognized as the community's cultural custodians, would share these tales during gatherings, using song, dance, and art to enhance the storytelling experience.

This oral tradition ensured not only the preservation of the stories but also maintained a living connection to the past. Even today, Dreamtime narratives are an intrinsic part of Aboriginal culture, echoing the voices of ancestors and keeping the spirit of the ancient world alive in the modern age.

Australian Aboriginal Dreamtime Stories are far more than just tales. They are a complex tapestry of history, spirituality, morality, and cultural identity. They remind us of the deep spiritual connection between humans and the natural world and highlight the rich tapestry of Indigenous culture that has thrived on the Australian continent for tens of thousands of years.

Chapter 5: Modern Scientific Techniques

In an age where science and technology intertwine more intimately than ever, our pursuit of self-awareness has been enhanced by pioneering methodologies and ground-breaking discoveries. Today, our understanding of the self isn't limited to ancient scriptures or philosophical treatises; it's complemented by a plethora of research and the rapid development of psychological and neurological tools.

Modern scientific techniques, in the realm of self-reflection, herald a convergence of age-old wisdom and cutting-edge science. They offer tangible, actionable, and often quantifiable insights into the depths of our minds and emotions. From understanding how our brain patterns affect our decision-making to leveraging cognitive methods to reshape harmful thought patterns, science has provided us with an arsenal of tools to help us know ourselves better.

This chapter delves deep into some of these ground-breaking techniques. We'll explore Neuro-Linguistic Programming (NLP), a method for aligning our subconscious and conscious thoughts; Cognitive Behavioral Therapy (CBT), which has revolutionized the way we address and rectify maladaptive behaviors; and Biofeedback, where real-time data about our body's functions provides feedback to enhance our physiological condition.

Together, these methodologies exemplify the strides humanity has taken in its perennial quest for self-understanding. So, whether you're a sceptic of the esoteric or an enthusiast eager to see where science meets the soul, embark on this journey through the corridors of contemporary knowledge and discover how it shapes the mirrors to our souls.

Neuro-Linguistic Programming (NLP)

Neuro-Linguistic Programming, commonly known as NLP, is an approach to communication, personal development, and psychotherapy. Developed in the 1970s by Richard Bandler and John Grinder, NLP posits that there is a relationship between neurological processes, language, and behavioral patterns that have been learned through experience. Essentially, it's believed that these can be changed to achieve specific goals in life.

Core Principles of NLP

One of the fundamental ideas in NLP is that the mind and body are interconnected. Our thoughts, feelings, and actions are all intertwined, and changes in one aspect can influence the others. A crucial tenet of NLP is that we all experience the world subjectively, meaning our perception of reality is based on our individual experiences and interpretations. This understanding acknowledges that people operate from their own map of the world, rather than a single objective reality.

Another key principle is the concept of modelling. Bandler and Grinder believed that if an individual excels in some activity, it's possible to model that behavior and teach it to others. This concept arose from their studies of individuals who were exceptionally talented in specific domains, like therapy or communication. By analysing and replicating their behaviors, strategies, and beliefs, they aimed to help others achieve similar success.

Techniques and Applications

NLP boasts a myriad of techniques aimed at enhancing communication, changing behaviors, setting goals, and resolving internal conflicts.

Some of the commonly used techniques include the "Swish Pattern" for changing unwanted behaviors, "Anchoring" for eliciting a particular state or emotion, and "Reframing" to change the way one perceives an event or experience.

NLP practitioners might work with individuals who want to overcome specific phobias, enhance their communication skills, or even improve their performance in areas like sports or business. It's also used in therapy sessions to help individuals confront and move past traumas or phobias, and it can be particularly effective for those looking to reshape negative thought patterns.

Controversies and Criticisms

While NLP has gained widespread popularity, it has also faced its share of criticisms. Some critics argue that NLP lacks empirical evidence and that its efficacy is anecdotal at best. Others assert that its foundational concepts are too vague and not clearly defined, making rigorous testing challenging. In the scientific community, the consensus is mixed, with some studies affirming the efficacy of certain NLP techniques and others disputing these claims.

Neuro-Linguistic Programming remains a compelling and influential approach in the realms of personal development, communication, and therapy. Whether or not one subscribes to all its principles, its emphasis on the power of language and thought in shaping our experiences offers valuable insights. As with any methodology, it's crucial to approach NLP with an open mind, seeking evidence-based practices and experienced practitioners when considering its application.

Cognitive Behavioral Therapy (CBT)

Cognitive Behavioral Therapy, commonly referred to as CBT, is a form of psychotherapeutic treatment that is geared towards helping individuals understand the interplay between their thoughts, feelings, and behaviors.

Rooted in the principles of cognitive and behavioral psychology, CBT posits that our thoughts can influence our feelings and behaviors, and by changing maladaptive thoughts, we can change our feelings and actions.

Historical Background:

CBT evolved from earlier forms of psychotherapy and can trace its origins back to the cognitive revolution of the 1960s.

Dr. Aaron T. Beck, often referred to as the father of CBT, observed that individuals suffering from depression held certain internal dialogues or "automatic thoughts" that contributed to their emotional distress.

He began focusing on these cognitive processes, paving the way for the development of CBT as a distinct therapeutic approach.

Core Principles:

Cognitive Processes: CBT emphasizes that it's not events themselves that upset us, but the meanings we give them. If our perception is skewed by cognitive distortions (such as overgeneralizing, catastrophizing, or black-and-white thinking), it can lead to emotional distress.

Behavioral Activation: Behavior and mood are interconnected. By changing behavior, especially behaviors that result from cognitive distortions, one can improve mood and overall well-being.

Activities like facing fears or engaging in mood-lifting actions are often integrated into CBT.

Skill Training: CBT often involves teaching individuals' various skills to manage their emotional and behavioral responses, such as stress-reduction techniques, problem-solving strategies, and assertiveness training.

Application:

CBT is a structured, goal-oriented therapy, often short-term in nature. It is used to treat a wide range of issues, from anxiety and depression to more complex disorders like obsessive-compulsive disorder (OCD) and post-traumatic stress disorder (PTSD). The therapy generally involves:

Assessment: Understanding the individual's specific concerns and how they manifest.

Identification of Negative Patterns: Recognizing harmful thought patterns or behaviors.

Reframing: Learning to challenge and change destructive thoughts or behaviors.

Homework Assignments: Practicing new strategies in real-life situations.

Benefits and Effectiveness:

CBT has been extensively researched and is considered one of the most effective therapeutic approaches, especially for anxiety and depressive disorders.

It offers practical skills that individuals can use in their daily lives, even after therapy concludes.

Its structured nature also means that it can be delivered in various formats, including individual sessions, group therapy, books, or online courses.

Limitations:

While CBT has proven effective for many individuals, it may not be suitable for everyone. Its structured and directive nature might not resonate with those who prefer a more explorative and open-ended therapy approach. Additionally, CBT primarily focuses on present thoughts and behaviors, which may not delve deep enough for individuals seeking to explore long-standing or deeply rooted issues from the past.

Cognitive Behavioral Therapy stands as a cornerstone in the realm of modern psychotherapy, offering a practical and evidence-based approach to address numerous psychological issues. By targeting the intricate dance between cognition and behavior, CBT equips individuals with tangible skills to reshape their perspective and, consequently, their life.

Biofeedback

Biofeedback is a therapeutic technique that trains individuals to control physiological functions using real-time data typically presented through auditory or visual signals. The term 'biofeedback' literally means 'life feedback,' underscoring the method's emphasis on providing immediate information about one's internal biological processes.

The primary objective of biofeedback is to enhance self-awareness and voluntary control over various physiological functions, thereby promoting better health and addressing specific conditions.

How Biofeedback Works

At its core, biofeedback is about monitoring bodily processes that are typically involuntary and using that information to gain control over them. During a biofeedback session, electronic sensors are attached to an individual's skin, which then relay information to a monitor.

This monitor displays real-time feedback, such as a beep, light, or graph, about bodily processes like heart rate, muscle tension, skin temperature, and brainwave patterns. By observing this feedback, individuals can learn to make subtle adjustments to their body, such as relaxing specific muscles or slowing their heart rate. Over time, with repeated sessions and training, individuals can learn to achieve these changes without the immediate feedback, gaining increased control over their physiological states.

Types of Biofeedback

There are various forms of biofeedback, each targeting a specific physiological function:

Electromyogram (EMG): This measures muscle tension. It's often used for conditions like anxiety, headaches, and back pain.

Thermal Biofeedback: By monitoring skin temperature, it can be used to treat conditions such as Raynaud's disease or migraine.

Neurofeedback or Electroencephalography (EEG): This observes brain wave patterns and can be beneficial in addressing conditions like ADHD, PTSD, or epilepsy.

Heart Rate Variability Biofeedback: This evaluates the variations in intervals between heartbeats and is helpful in managing stress or anxiety.

Respiratory Biofeedback: This monitor breathing patterns and rate, proving beneficial for conditions like asthma.

Applications and Benefits

Biofeedback has been utilized in managing a wide array of health issues. These include chronic pain, migraines, stress, anxiety disorders, hypertension, and certain respiratory ailments.

Moreover, athletes and performers sometimes use biofeedback to improve concentration and performance by learning to maintain a calm and focused physiological state. One of the primary benefits of biofeedback is that it's non-invasive, offering a drug-free alternative or complementary option to conventional treatments.

Limitations and Considerations

While biofeedback is a valuable tool with numerous applications, it's not a magic bullet. Not everyone responds to it in the same way, and its effectiveness varies from person to person.

It's essential for individuals to approach biofeedback with realistic expectations and understand that it's a skill that requires practice and patience. Additionally, while biofeedback can be used independently, it's often most effective when combined with other therapeutic interventions, such as cognitive-behavioral therapy.

In summary, biofeedback is a pioneering technique that bridges the gap between our physiological and psychological worlds, empowering individuals to achieve better health and well-being by gaining insights and control over their internal processes.

Chapter 6: The Role of Art and Creativity

Across the canvas of history, art has always served as a mirror to the human soul. It encapsulates our deepest emotions, desires, and questions about our existence. Beyond its aesthetic appeal, art in its many forms, be it visual, musical, or literary, has profound transformative abilities that can help individuals delve deeper into the realms of self-awareness and reflection.

In this chapter, we will explore the intimate relationship between art, creativity, and self-reflection. From the cathartic strokes of a painter's brush to the evocative verses of a poet, art serves as both a medium for expression and a tool for introspection. It offers a safe space where one can externalize internal struggles, leading to profound insights about oneself and the world around.

Creativity, often interlinked with artistic pursuits, is not just the reserve of the 'gifted'. It is an inherent trait within all of us, waiting to be harnessed. By indulging in creative acts, individuals can unlock suppressed emotions, re-evaluate life perspectives, and even discover previously unrecognized aspects of their personality.

As we traverse through this chapter, readers will be introduced to various artistic mediums and their therapeutic potentials. We'll delve into real-life accounts of individuals who've embarked on transformative journeys through their artistic endeavors and provide practical techniques to integrate art and creativity into one's self-reflective practices.

Join us on this illuminating journey, and discover how art and creativity can serve as powerful lenses, providing clearer, more vivid reflections of the soul.

Painting and Drawing as a Form of Self-Exploration

Historical Context: For millennia, humans have been painting and drawing as both a method of expression and a tool for introspection. Cave paintings from prehistoric times not only served as historical records but were also likely tools for spiritual and emotional exploration. Renaissance artists, in their pursuit of perfection and beauty, regularly delved into the human psyche to produce artworks that resonated with emotional depth.

The Canvas as a Safe Space: Engaging with a blank canvas or sheet of paper can be akin to engaging with one's own inner world. This space allows for uninhibited expression, without the confines of language or the constraints of societal judgment. For many, the act of laying down paint or pencil marks is therapeutic because it provides an immediate, tangible outlet for internal feelings and thoughts.

Beyond Representation: While representational artwork can be cathartic, especially when portraying personal experiences or memories, abstract art offers a unique avenue for emotional exploration. The colors, shapes, and forms in abstract artwork often emanate directly from the artist's current emotional state, subconscious thoughts, or unresolved tensions. They don't necessarily depict a 'real' scene but are instead a visceral representation of the inner landscape of the artist.

The Process Matters: Often, it's not just the final piece of artwork that offers insight and healing, but the very act of painting or drawing. The rhythmic motion of the brush or pencil, the merging of colors, and the evolving image on the canvas can be meditative. This immersion in the creative process can lead to a state of 'flow', where time seems to disappear, and one is fully engaged in the moment. This state not only alleviates stress but can also bring forth buried emotions or thoughts to the conscious mind.

Tools for Self-Discovery: Art therapists often use painting and drawing as tools for helping individuals delve into their subconscious. The artworks produced can serve as points of discussion, revealing hidden fears, traumas, desires, or dreams. For instance, the choice of colors can offer insights into one's emotional state, dark, muted colors might represent melancholy or depression, while bright, vibrant hues could indicate joy, energy, or optimism.

Inclusivity of the Medium: One of the most beautiful aspects of painting and drawing is that they are inclusive. One doesn't need to be a trained artist to use these mediums for self-exploration. Even simple doodles or splashes of paint can be deeply revealing. The emphasis isn't on producing 'good' art, but rather on the process of creation and the insights it can bring.

Painting and drawing, in their essence, are not just about creating beautiful or thought-provoking images. They are windows into the soul, offering both the artist and the viewer a glimpse into the myriad emotions, thoughts, and experiences that make up the human experience. Embracing these mediums for personal exploration can lead to profound insights, healing, and a deeper connection with one's authentic self.

Creative Writing

Creative writing is the art of crafting stories, poems, plays, and other narrative forms using the imagination and creativity of the writer. Unlike technical, academic, journalistic, or other forms of writing, the primary purpose of creative writing is to entertain and evoke emotion. It's a form of expression that delves into the human experience, capturing moments of significance, whether they be profound or everyday encounters.

The Genres of Creative Writing

There are myriad genres within creative writing, each with its own set of conventions and characteristics. Some of the most popular include fiction (encompassing everything from short stories to full-length novels), poetry (ranging from sonnets to free verse), drama (plays, screenplays, and teleplays), and creative non-fiction (where factual narratives are presented with literary styles).

Additionally, genres like fantasy, science fiction, romance, horror, and crime fiction are subcategories within the broader fiction classification, each appealing to different tastes and interests.

Benefits of Creative Writing

Creative writing offers writers a platform to express themselves, delve into their innermost thoughts, beliefs, and feelings, and share them with the world. It can be therapeutic, allowing writers to process experiences, ideas, and emotions. Additionally, creative writing sharpens critical thinking, improves vocabulary, and fosters a deep understanding of the intricacies of language.

It also builds empathy in writers, as they often have to see the world from various perspectives to create believable characters and scenarios.

The Process of Creative Writing

The journey of creative writing often begins with a spark – an idea, a feeling, or a vision. From this initial inspiration, writers draft their narratives, continually refining through revisions. Along the way, many writers rely on tools like character development sheets, plot diagrams, and mood boards to shape their work.

Feedback is also a crucial component of the creative process. Whether from writing groups, editors, or peers, critiques can offer insights and suggestions to elevate a piece from good to great.

Creative Writing in Contemporary Culture

In today's digital age, the scope of creative writing has expanded tremendously. While traditional forms like books and plays remain popular, the internet has given rise to new platforms such as blogs, podcasts, and online literary magazines.

Social media platforms, particularly Twitter and Instagram, have birthed micro-fiction and poetry trends. With technology's aid, storytelling has also evolved, leading to interactive narratives in video games and virtual reality experiences.

Challenges and Triumphs of Creative Writing

Like any art form, creative writing comes with its set of challenges. Writer's block, criticism, and the daunting task of getting published are just a few hurdles many writers face. Yet, the joys of writing, of creating worlds, characters, and stories from mere thoughts, far outweigh the challenges.

The thrill of seeing one's work in print, receiving feedback from readers, or simply the personal satisfaction of having penned a story, poem, or play makes the journey worthwhile.

In essence, creative writing is a celebration of the human spirit, a testament to the boundless limits of imagination, and an exploration into the depths of human emotions and experiences.

Whether one is a seasoned author or a budding writer, the world of creative writing offers a canvas to paint stories that can captivate, inspire, and resonate with readers across time and space.

Music and Dance

A Reflection of the Human Spirit

Music has always been a profound expression of human emotion and thought. Since the dawn of humanity, our ancestors have used it as a means to communicate, to celebrate, and to mourn.

It transcends languages and can evoke powerful emotions in people regardless of their background. Music is not just an arrangement of notes and melodies; it's a universal language that speaks to our souls. It has the power to calm the anxious mind, energize the weary, and bring tears to the eyes.

Whether it's the gentle strumming of a guitar, the robust tones of a symphony, or the intricate rhythms of a drum, music taps into our innermost feelings, often expressing what words cannot. Listening to music can also be a deep form of self-reflection.

The lyrics of a song might resonate with one's personal experiences, or the melody might transport someone back to a specific time or memory. In therapeutic contexts, music has been used to aid in emotional release, memory recall, and as a tool for relaxation and stress reduction.

Dance, on the other hand, is music made visible. It is the physical expression of what one feels when they hear a tune.

From the disciplined movements of ballet to the free-flowing forms of contemporary dance, from the energetic leaps of hip-hop to the poised elegance of ballroom – dance is a celebration of the human body's ability to move, tell a story, and reflect emotions.

Cultures around the world have their unique dance forms, each telling a story about their history, values, and beliefs.

For many, dance is a way to connect with their roots, understand their past, and express their individual and collective identities. Moreover, dance, much like music, offers therapeutic benefits. Dance therapy, as a discipline, explores the idea that motion and emotion are interconnected.

It uses dance as a medium to promote emotional, social, cognitive, and physical integration. By engaging in dance, individuals often find a safe space to explore and express feelings they might not be able to articulate verbally.

Together, music and dance form a symbiotic relationship where one complements the other. They provide a holistic experience that engages both the mind and body, allowing individuals to express and reflect upon their innermost feelings, memories, and aspirations.

In many ways, they are mirrors to the soul, offering glimpses into the vast spectrum of human emotions and experiences. Whether you're a listener or a performer, engaging with music and dance can be a deeply transformative experience, grounding us in the present and connecting us with the rhythms of life.

Chapter 7: Technology and Self-Reflection

In the ever-evolving digital age, technology has permeated every corner of our lives. From the smartphones we clutch in our hands to the smart devices dotting our homes and offices, there's no escaping its profound influence.

Yet, amidst the barrage of notifications, endless social media scrolls, and the constant beckoning of screen glow, lies an opportunity. Technology, often criticized for distancing us from our true selves, can also be harnessed as a powerful tool for introspection and self-growth.

The marriage of technology and self-reflection might seem paradoxical at first. On one hand, there's the age-old practice of introspection, often associated with silent retreats, meditation cushions, and serene natural surroundings.

On the other, there's the futuristic world of technology, with its relentless pace and sometimes intrusive nature. However, when channeled correctly, technology can serve as a mirror, offering us clear reflections of our innermost thoughts, feelings, and patterns.

This chapter delves into the synergistic intersection of technology and self-reflection. We'll explore various digital tools, apps, and platforms that have been designed to facilitate deeper understanding and awareness of oneself.

From journaling applications that help catalogue our thoughts to virtual reality therapies transporting us to worlds that trigger profound insights, technology holds a myriad of possibilities for those on a journey of self-discovery.

As we journey through this chapter, let's keep an open mind. Let's challenge the preconceived notion that screens distance us from our souls. Instead, let's explore how they can become windows to our innermost selves, aiding us in the eternal quest for self-awareness in this digital age.

Tools for Journaling

Journaling is a time-honored tradition that has evolved alongside advancements in technology. Today's journaling tools range from the classic pen and paper to innovative digital platforms that incorporate multimedia. These tools cater to a diverse range of preferences, providing everyone a unique method to document their thoughts, experiences, and personal growth.

Traditional Paper Journals:

Bound Notebooks: Classic tools that never go out of style, leather-bound or hardcover notebooks provide a tactile experience many writers appreciate.

Benefits:

Physical interaction can be therapeutic.

No digital distractions.

Can be personalized with sketches, doodles, or stickers.

Printable Journal Templates: Available online, these templates provide structured prompts and designs that users can print and fill out.

Benefits:

Provides structure for those unsure of how to start.

Can be customized to fit specific themes (gratitude, travel, etc.).

Economical and easily replaceable.

Digital Journaling Tools:

Dedicated Journaling Apps: These are applications built explicitly for journaling. Examples include Day One, Penzu, and Journey.

Benefits:

Sync across multiple devices.

Incorporate multimedia like photos, videos, and voice notes.

Often include security features like password protection or encryption.

Blogging Platforms: Websites like WordPress, Medium, or Blogger offer platforms for people who prefer sharing their journal entries with an audience.

Benefits:

Potential for community interaction.

Flexible formatting options.

Ability to reach a wider audience and receive feedback.

Cloud-Based Note-Taking Apps: Applications such as Evernote or Microsoft OneNote can be adapted for journaling purposes.

Benefits:

Highly customizable organization with notebooks, tags, and categories.

Accessible from any device with cloud syncing.

Allows for collaboration if users wish to share entries with specific individuals.

Multimedia Options:

Video Journaling: With platforms like YouTube or Vimeo, individuals can record and store video diaries.

Benefits:

Captures facial expressions, voice modulations, and settings.

Offers a different dimension of personal reflection.

Can be made public or kept private based on user preference.

Voice Journaling: Tools like Otter.ai or simple voice recording apps allow users to speak their entries.

Benefits:

Perfect for those who think aloud or don't like typing/writing.

Can be transcribed into text if needed.

Ideal for capturing thoughts on the go.

Selecting the right tool for journaling largely depends on personal preference, comfort with technology, and the desired outcome of the journaling process. It's essential to experiment and find the tool or combination of tools that resonate most with one's journaling goals.

Dive Deeper into Self-Discovery with Our Latest Release!

Do you ever find yourself seeking clarity about who you truly are? Yearning to uncover deeper truths hidden beneath the surface of daily life? Our newest journal is crafted just for you!

Introducing:

The Introspection Journal: 365 Prompts to Understand Yourself

Why this journal is a MUST-HAVE:

Personal Growth: Unlock insights about your beliefs, dreams, emotions, and more.

Daily Reflection: A structured, year-long journey through thought-provoking prompts.

Enhanced Self-Awareness: Discover patterns, embrace growth, and achieve greater clarity in your life decisions.

Whether you're a seasoned journaler or just beginning your journey, this journal promises a transformative experience. Each prompt is designed to guide you deeper into your mind, heart, and soul. Embrace the opportunity to become your own best friend, confidant, and guide.

Embark on a journey of introspection and self-love. Claim your journal today and embrace the beauty of true self-awareness!

Get it now at

InspirationDB.com/Journal

Virtual Reality Therapy (VRT)

Virtual Reality Therapy (VRT), sometimes known as Virtual Reality Exposure Therapy (VRET), is a form of treatment that uses virtual reality technology to expose patients to simulations of real-world environments or situations that they might find distressing. These controlled and safe virtual environments help individuals confront and process problematic situations under the guidance of a trained therapist. VRT is particularly recognized for its potential in treating phobias, post-traumatic stress disorder (PTSD), and anxiety disorders, among other conditions.

How It Works:

Controlled Exposure: In VRT, patients are gradually and systematically exposed to their fear triggers in a virtual environment. The gradual exposure helps to desensitize patients to the trigger, thereby reducing associated distress and anxiety.

Real-time Feedback: Therapists can monitor a patient's physiological responses (like heart rate or perspiration) in real-time, offering immediate intervention or adjustment to the therapy as necessary.

Flexibility: The virtual scenarios can be tailored to each patient's specific needs, ensuring that the therapy is both effective and individualized.

Advantages:

Safety: VRT allows individuals to confront their fears in a controlled and risk-free environment. Privacy: For patients who may be embarrassed or hesitant about confronting their fears in real life, VRT offers a private alternative.

Convenience: With advancements in VR technology, VRT can sometimes be conducted from the comfort of one's home, making therapy more accessible.

Efficiency: Research indicates that VRT can often achieve quicker results compared to traditional therapeutic methods due to its immersive nature.

Applications:

Phobias: From fear of flying to fear of spiders, VRT can replicate the triggering situations for a variety of phobias.

PTSD: VRT has been used to help war veterans confront traumatic war-time scenarios in a controlled setting to reduce associated trauma.

Anxiety Disorders: Scenarios that might induce panic attacks or other anxiety responses can be recreated in VR, allowing patients to develop coping mechanisms.

Challenges:

Technology Limitations: While VR tech has advanced considerably, there can still be limitations in perfectly replicating real-world situations.

Physical Side Effects: Some people might experience dizziness, nausea, or disorientation while using VR.

Accessibility: High-quality VR setups can be expensive, potentially limiting access for some patients.

Virtual Reality Therapy presents an exciting confluence of technology and therapy. As VR technology continues to improve and become more accessible, its applications in therapeutic settings will likely expand, offering innovative treatments for a range of conditions.

Online Self-Awareness Courses and Webinars

In an increasingly digital world, the realm of personal development and self-awareness has seamlessly transitioned onto online platforms, allowing individuals to embark on journeys of self-discovery from the comfort of their homes.

This digital shift has particularly manifested in the form of online self-awareness courses and webinars, which have become powerful tools for those seeking deeper insights into their own psyche, behaviors, and patterns.

Online Self-Awareness Courses: These are structured, often modular programs designed to guide participants through a series of lessons, exercises, and assignments cantered around understanding oneself better.

The flexibility they offer is invaluable. Unlike traditional classroom settings, participants can move at their own pace, revisiting challenging topics or skipping those they're familiar with. Many of these courses incorporate a mix of videos, reading materials, interactive quizzes, and reflective journaling assignments.

Some popular courses even offer certification upon completion, making it a valuable addition for professionals in counselling, coaching, or leadership roles. Another notable advantage of online courses is the access to a global community.

Many platforms have forums or discussion boards where participants from around the world can share insights, experiences, and offer peer support, enriching the learning experience.

Webinars: Webinars, or web-based seminars, bring the live seminar experience to one's computer or smartphone screen. Typically led by experts or thought leaders in the field of personal development, these sessions often focus on specific aspects of self-awareness, be it emotional intelligence, mindfulness techniques, or deep-diving into personality types.

Unlike courses, webinars are generally real-time events, making them more dynamic and interactive. Attendees can often ask questions, participate in live polls, or engage in breakout group discussions.

This real-time interaction offers a unique advantage, the immediacy of feedback and the sense of being part of a live event can be immensely motivating for many. Furthermore, many webinars are recorded, allowing registered participants to revisit the content later or catch up if they missed the live session.

In conclusion, online self-awareness courses and webinars are revolutionizing the way we approach personal growth. They democratize access to expert knowledge, offer unprecedented flexibility, and create global communities bound by the shared goal of self-discovery.

Whether you're a beginner just starting on your self-awareness journey or a seasoned practitioner, there's likely an online course or webinar tailored to your needs and interests. As with all digital resources, however, it's essential to vet the credibility of the platform and the expertise of the instructors to ensure a beneficial and authentic learning experience.

Chapter 8: Case Studies

In our journey through the myriad techniques and philosophies of self-reflection, we've journeyed across continents, through time, and into the depths of human cognition. Yet, while theory and technique are vital components to understanding, sometimes the true essence of a practice is best understood through real-life experiences. Stories have a unique power to illuminate the abstract, making complex concepts palpable and deeply personal.

In this chapter, we delve into the lived experiences of individuals from different walks of life who have engaged with various self-reflection practices, both ancient and modern. These case studies serve as a testament to the transformative power of self-awareness and offer insights into the tangible outcomes one can expect from dedicated introspection.

Whether it's the tale of a businessman finding clarity in the serene practices of Eastern mindfulness, a struggling artist reconnecting with her roots through Indigenous ceremonies, or a tech-savvy teenager harnessing modern apps for self-exploration, these stories underscore a universal truth: the quest for self-understanding is both deeply personal and universally human.

As you immerse yourself in these narratives, may you find inspiration, draw parallels to your own life, and gather the motivation to embark on your own self-reflective journey, armed with the knowledge that the path to self-awareness is as diverse as humanity itself.

Personal stories and interviews that showcase the effectiveness of different techniques

1. Sarah: Finding Solace in Journaling

Narrative:

Sarah was a busy corporate lawyer, often overwhelmed by the mounting pressure. However, her life took a turn when she stumbled upon a journaling workshop. Initially skeptical, she soon realized that this was her escape and mirror to her thoughts. Every night, she'd write down her emotions, challenges, and small wins.

Interview Excerpt:

"Before journaling, I'd internalize my stress. But once I began pouring my thoughts onto paper, it was like a weight lifted. The pages held my anxieties, and over time, patterns emerged. I learned my triggers and also the things that brought joy. It's a technique so simple, yet profoundly transformative."

2. Aman: Dancing His Worries Away

Narrative:

Growing up in a traditional family, Aman always found it hard to express himself. But dance, especially the spontaneous kind, became his refuge. Whenever he felt lost or overwhelmed, he'd lock his room and dance, letting his body channel his emotions.

Interview Excerpt:

"Dance became my language. In moments of despair, confusion, or even sheer happiness, my body knew how to articulate those emotions. It was a process of introspection, where every move, every beat resonated with what I felt inside. I didn't need words; my dance was my reflection."

3. Javier: Embracing Mindfulness in the Digital Age

Narrative:

Javier was a tech enthusiast, always updated with the latest apps and gadgets. When he encountered an app on mindfulness meditation, his curiosity was piqued. He began with just 5 minutes a day, gradually increasing his sessions. This digital intervention became his tool for grounding.

Interview Excerpt:

"It's ironic, you know? We often blame technology for our distractions, but here I was, using the same technology for self-awareness. Those meditation sessions, guided by the app, made me more present. I'd be more attentive in conversations, savor my meals, and generally, life seemed more vivid. It's a modern technique, but its roots are ancient, and I believe that's what makes it powerful."

4. Mei: Rediscovering Roots through Indigenous Ceremonies

Narrative:

Mei, a third-generation immigrant, often felt disconnected from her cultural roots.

On a trip back to her ancestral homeland, she participated in a traditional tea ceremony, which locals described as a form of introspection and connection. The ceremony, spanning over hours, required patience, precision, and presence.

Interview Excerpt:

"Every pour, every sip, every moment in the ceremony was steeped in history and symbolism. As the hours went by, I felt a connection – not just to my ancestors but to myself.

It was as if the act of slowing down, savoring, and being present allowed me to bridge a gap I didn't know existed. It wasn't just about the tea; it was about understanding where I came from and where I am now."

5. Elias: Nature Walks and the Art of Observation

Narrative:

Elias, a biology teacher from Sweden, had always been passionate about nature. For him, the simple act of taking a walk in the woods was a self-reflective journey. He would observe the minutest details: the patterns on a leaf, the ripple of water, or the flight of a bird.

Interview Excerpt:

"Nature, in all its complexity, mirrors our own lives. When I'm out in the woods, I'm not just observing nature; I'm reflecting on my own life. How am I adapting?

What patterns am I following? Nature has this uncanny ability to make you ask questions about your own existence and choices. It's therapy in the purest form."

6. Rhea: The Power of Sound Meditation

Narrative:

Rhea, a sound engineer, came across the concept of sound baths and sound meditation. Given her profession, she was intrigued. She attended a session where gongs, bowls, and chimes were used. The resonance and vibrations had a profound effect on her.

Interview Excerpt:

"Being in a room filled with vibrations that you can literally feel coursing through you is surreal. It's like the sound waves were pushing out all my anxieties, doubts, and stress. I left feeling lighter, more attuned to myself. Now, I not only attend sessions but have integrated sound meditation into my daily life. It's a reminder of how sometimes, the external can guide us deeper into our internal worlds."

7. Faiza: Grappling with Grief through Art Therapy

Narrative:

Faiza, having lost her younger brother in a tragic accident, felt trapped in a spiral of grief and depression. On a friend's recommendation, she began attending art therapy sessions. Through colors, strokes, and forms, she expressed her pain, love, and memories.

Interview Excerpt:

"Words often failed me. How could they encapsulate such profound grief? But when I painted, it was as if my soul was speaking. The canvas captured my brother's smile, our shared memories, my anguish, and eventually, my journey to healing. Art became both my refuge and my mirror."

8. Leo: Tai Chi and the Dance of Awareness

Narrative:

Leo, once a professional sprinter, faced a career-ending injury that forced him into early retirement. Battling resentment and a loss of identity, he chanced upon Tai Chi – a martial art emphasizing slow movements and deep breathing. It became his path to physical recovery and mental clarity.

Interview Excerpt:

"In sprinting, it was always about speed. With Tai Chi, I learned the power of slowness and deliberation. Each movement required presence and balance. It not only helped me rehabilitate physically but made me introspect on the impermanence of life and the importance of resilience."

9. Nandini: Harnessing the Power of Guided Imagery

Narrative:

Nandini, a young entrepreneur, often felt overwhelmed by the challenges of running a start-up. She discovered guided imagery sessions, where visualization techniques were used to navigate stress. The scenarios crafted in her mind's eye provided solace and clarity.

Interview Excerpt:

"The mind is a powerful tool. Through guided imagery, I'd often visualize a serene beach or a mountain summit. These mental escapades weren't just breaking; they became strategy sessions. I'd often find solutions to business challenges during these visualizations. It was as if my subconscious mind was working things out in these peaceful settings."

10. Kaya: Healing through Nature Retreats

Narrative:

Kaya, a software developer constantly glued to screens, felt a growing sense of disconnection with herself and the world around her. On a whim, she signed up for a week-long nature retreat, exchanging urban landscapes for serene mountains and forests.

Interview Excerpt:

"I never realized how much the constant buzz of the city and the blue light of screens had affected me until I spent a week in nature. The retreat wasn't just about disconnecting from technology, but reconnecting with myself. The chirping birds, rustling leaves, and tranquil waters spoke to me, reminding me of life's simple pleasures and my place in the vast tapestry of nature."

11. Carlos: Embracing Stillness with Vipassana Meditation

Narrative:

Carlos, a schoolteacher, always felt a sense of unrest, constantly seeking more from life. A colleague introduced him to Vipassana – a 10-day silent meditation retreat. No talking, reading, or writing; just him and his thoughts.

Interview Excerpt:

"Those ten days were the hardest and most enlightening of my life. In the silence, I confronted my fears, regrets, joys, and hopes. By the end, I emerged with a clearer understanding of my desires and a deeper appreciation for the present. Vipassana taught me that sometimes, you find the most profound insights in the depths of silence."

12. Lina: Building Self-Awareness through Group Therapy

Narrative:

Lina, struggling with feelings of isolation and self-doubt, decided to join a group therapy session on a friend's suggestion. Sharing and listening to others' experiences in a safe environment turned out to be her path to understanding herself better.

Interview Excerpt:

"At first, I was apprehensive about sharing my innermost feelings with strangers. But as the sessions went on, I realized that many of us shared similar struggles. Hearing others articulate their feelings often gave words to my own emotions. The group became a mirror, reflecting aspects of myself I had been unaware of. Through our shared journeys, I discovered my own."

13. Ashwin: Transformation through Fasting and Self-Inquiry

Narrative:

Ashwin, a successful restaurateur, found himself engrossed in the pleasures of life, often feeling satiated yet empty inside. Intrigued by ancient fasting rituals, he embarked on a 3-day fast, not just from food, but from his regular life, using the time for self-inquiry.

Interview Excerpt:

"The hunger pangs were intense, but they paled in comparison to the mental clarity I achieved. As my body detoxified, so did my mind. In the quiet moments, I asked myself hard questions about my purpose, ambitions, and the legacy I wanted to leave. Fasting was not just a physical cleanse but a spiritual reboot."

14. Odette: Exploration through Dream Analysis

Narrative:

Odette, a novelist facing writer's block, turned to her dreams for inspiration. Keeping a dream journal by her bedside, she began recording and analysing her dreams, unearthing hidden fears, desires, and memories.

Interview Excerpt:

"My dreams were like abstract paintings, sometimes vivid, sometimes blurry. Analysing them was like piecing together a puzzle. I realized many of my dreams mirrored unresolved issues or suppressed desires. This exploration not only refueled my writing but also gave me profound insights into my subconscious mind."

15. Jamal: Navigating Life with Stoic Philosophy

Narrative:

Jamal, a community leader, often felt the weight of responsibility and the volatility of societal issues. He chanced upon Stoic philosophy, applying its principles of control, acceptance, and virtue to navigate life's challenges.

Interview Excerpt:

"Stoicism taught me to differentiate between what I could control and what I couldn't. I learned to embrace challenges, view them as opportunities for growth, and maintain equanimity. It was a centuries-old philosophy, but its relevance in today's chaotic world was astonishing. It became my compass, guiding me through storms with resilience and grace."

16. Isabella: Harnessing Creativity with Mindful Crafting

Narrative:

Isabella, a graphic designer, often felt disconnected from her creations because of the relentless pace of digital work. She turned to mindful crafting, be it knitting, pottery, or simple doodling, as a means of tangible self-expression and meditation.

Interview Excerpt:

"Crafting gave me the tactile experience I missed in the digital realm. Every stitch in knitting, every curve in pottery became a deliberate act of mindfulness. It grounded me, allowing my creativity to flow naturally and helping me find peace in the act of creation itself."

17. Darius: Echoes of the Past through Ancestral Exploration

Narrative:

Darius, intrigued by family tales of migration and endurance, delved into genealogical research. Unearthing stories of ancestors, understanding their challenges, and celebrating their victories became a mirror to his own strengths and vulnerabilities.

Interview Excerpt:

"The more I learned about my ancestors, the clearer my own reflection became. Their stories of perseverance, love, and ambition resonated deeply, making me realize the legacy I carried within. This journey through time not only connected me to my roots but also helped shape my vision for the future."

18. Amara: Introspection through Silence Retreats

Narrative:

Amara, an event planner constantly surrounded by noise and demands, felt an urge to experience silence. She enrolled in a silence retreat, spending days without speaking, allowing the stillness to amplify her inner voice.

Interview Excerpt:

"In the absence of external noise, my internal dialogue became louder. Initially, it was overwhelming, confronting thoughts I'd pushed away. But as days passed, the chaos settled into clarity. The retreat was more than just silence; it was an opportunity to truly listen to myself, to understand my desires, fears, and dreams."

Every individual, in their pursuit of self-awareness, chooses a path that resonates deeply with their essence. These stories and experiences illuminate the infinite avenues available to discover oneself. Each journey, unique in its approach, converges on the universal human yearning for connection, understanding, and growth. These narratives are testament to the adaptability and resilience of the human spirit, always seeking, always evolving.

Chapter 9: Creating Your Personalized Self-Reflection Plan

In the tapestry of life, no two threads are identical. Similarly, when it comes to the intimate journey of self-reflection, there's no one-size-fits-all. What works wonders for one might barely scratch the surface for another.

The beauty of self-reflection lies in its adaptability, allowing us to draw from various traditions, techniques, and teachings to create a path uniquely suited to our individual nature.

Throughout this book, we've traversed the vast landscape of self-reflection techniques, from time-honored Eastern philosophies to modern scientific methods. We've explored practices deeply rooted in cultural traditions and dabbled in the potential of cutting-edge technologies. As we stand at this juncture, the key question arises: How can you weave these threads of wisdom into a coherent, personalized tapestry of self-awareness?

This chapter is your guide to doing just that. We'll delve into the process of assessing your own inclinations and needs, understanding which techniques resonate most with you, and crafting a plan that not only aligns with your daily routine but also nourishes your soul.

More than just a set of instructions, this chapter is an invitation, to take ownership of your journey, to celebrate your uniqueness, and to embark on a path of self-reflection that truly mirrors the depths of your soul.

So, let's begin this final chapter with a sense of curiosity, openness, and the understanding that your journey is yours alone, waiting to be charted.

Assessing Your Needs and Preferences

Self-awareness begins with understanding our unique needs and preferences. This knowledge is pivotal because it acts as a guidepost for making decisions that resonate with our inner selves. It's not just about understanding who you are, but also about recognizing what makes you tick, what fuels your passions, and what dims your light. It's a journey that requires honesty, vulnerability, and time.

Assessing Needs:

Personal Values Assessment: Begin by determining what values hold utmost importance for you.

Is it family, financial freedom, creativity, or perhaps integrity?

Understand what lies at the core of your decisions.

Lifestyle Evaluation: Examine your current lifestyle.

What aspects of it are in sync with your true self?

Which parts seem out of alignment?

Emotional and Physical Needs: It's also important to recognize what you need emotionally and physically to thrive.

Do you need regular social interaction, or do you thrive in solitude?

Is physical activity a necessity for your well-being or is calm, meditative practice more your style?

Determining Preferences:

Activity Preferences: Reflect on the activities that make you lose track of time.

Do you enjoy reading, hiking, painting, or perhaps coding?

What hobbies or tasks make you feel invigorated?

Learning Styles: We all have distinct ways we learn best.

Some people are visual learners, while others are auditory or kinesthetics.

Recognizing this can help you approach new information or skills more efficiently.

Social Interactions: Think about your social preferences.

Do large groups energize you, or do they drain your energy?

Do you prefer deep, meaningful one-on-one conversations or light, group interactions?

Work Environment: Your productivity and satisfaction at work are often linked to the environment and work style.

Do you prefer a structured, office setting or a flexible, remote arrangement?

Do you thrive under clear guidance, or do you prefer autonomy in your tasks?

Assessing your needs and preferences isn't a one-time task. As you grow and evolve, these may shift. Regularly checking in with yourself ensures that you remain in alignment with your true self, helping you lead a more fulfilling life. Whether it's a career choice, a hobby, or even daily routines, understanding your needs and preferences ensures that your choices reflect who you truly are.

Step-by-step guide to creating a personalized plan

Understanding Your Needs and Preferences

Before diving into any plan, it's crucial to understand why you're doing it and what you hope to gain.

Assessment:

Start by assessing your current level of self-awareness. Are there specific areas in your life that require more clarity?

Identify triggers or challenges that often prompt introspection or cause you to feel disconnected from your core.

Desired Outcomes:

Write down what you aim to achieve. This could range from understanding your emotional triggers to identifying your life's purpose or even small daily insights.

By knowing your 'why', you'll stay motivated and connected to the process.

Choosing Techniques That Resonate

With numerous techniques available from different cultures and philosophies, it's essential to pick those that align with you.

Research:

Explore various techniques discussed earlier in the book, or even venture outside for other methodologies.

Look for first hand experiences or reviews from people who have tried these techniques.

Experiment:

Before committing, try out a few methods to see which ones feel right. For instance, if journaling appeals to you, spend a week writing daily reflections.

Remember that what works for one person might not work for another, so stay open-minded and patient.

Creating a Schedule

Consistency is key when it comes to self-reflection.

Determine Frequency:

Decide if you want to practice daily, weekly, or at any other regular interval. The more frequent, the better, but it's vital to remain realistic about what you can commit to.

Set Aside Specific Times:

Designate specific times in your day or week for self-reflection. For many, early mornings or evenings work best as they provide quiet moments for introspection.

Setting reminders or alarms can help you stay on track.

Monitoring and Adjusting

Growth is an ongoing process, and your needs might change over time.

Review Periodically:

Set aside time, perhaps once a month or quarterly, to review your insights and see if you're moving towards your desired outcomes.

Adjust Techniques:

If a technique isn't providing the insights or growth you'd hoped for, don't hesitate to try something else. Your self-reflection journey is deeply personal and can evolve over time.

Seeking External Feedback

Sometimes, the view from outside can offer invaluable insights.

Trusted Friends and Family:

Occasionally, discuss your reflections and insights with close friends or family. They can offer perspectives you might not have considered.

Professional Guidance:

If you feel stuck or overwhelmed, consider seeking a coach, counsellor, or therapist to guide you deeper into your self-reflection journey.

Maintaining a Record

Documenting your journey can provide clarity and show how far you've come.

Journal or Digital Tool:

Whether you prefer pen and paper or digital tools, maintain a record of your reflections, insights, and growth.

Review Milestones:

Every now and then, look back at your entries to observe patterns, growth, or recurring themes. It can be incredibly insightful to see your evolution over time.

Embarking on a journey of self-reflection is a brave and transformative step. This plan, though detailed, is just a starting point. It's essential to stay attuned to your inner voice, adjust when necessary, and celebrate the insights and growth along the way.

Tips for Maintaining Consistency

Consistency is the bedrock upon which successful habits are built. Whether you're embarking on a new fitness routine, trying to cultivate a meditation practice, or diving into deep self-reflection as outlined in "Mirrors to the Soul," maintaining consistency can often be the most challenging aspect. Here are some actionable tips to help you cultivate and maintain a consistent approach to any endeavor:

Set Clear Intentions:

Purpose Over Preference: Before starting any habit or routine, understand the 'why' behind it. When your intention is tied to a deeper purpose, it's easier to stay consistent, even on days when you don't 'feel' like it.

Write it Down: Documenting your intentions can be a powerful motivator. Seeing your goals in black and white can provide a daily reminder of what you're aiming for.

Create a Routine:

Scheduled Time Blocks: Allocate specific times during your day for your chosen activity. Treating it as an essential appointment can prevent other obligations from taking precedence.

Same Time, Same Place: Whenever possible, carry out your activity at the same time and place every day. This helps in developing muscle memory and turning your task into a daily ritual.

Start Small and Gradually Increase:

Baby Steps: Beginning with smaller, more manageable goals can prevent feelings of being overwhelmed. For example, if you're trying to cultivate a reading habit, start with just five minutes a day.

Progressive Overload: Once you feel comfortable, gradually increase your commitment. This could mean reading for longer periods, intensifying your workout, or delving deeper into self-reflection techniques.

Hold Yourself Accountable:

Track Your Progress: Use tools, apps, or plain old journals to track your daily activities. This not only gives a sense of accomplishment but also highlights any inconsistency.

Find an Accountability Partner: Sharing your goals with a friend or joining a group with similar objectives can provide the necessary external motivation to stay on track.

Forgive and Re-align:

Avoid the All-or-Nothing Mindset: Missed a day or two? It's okay. Instead of getting discouraged or giving up entirely, simply refocus and continue from where you left off.

Self-compassion: Understand that being consistent doesn't mean being perfect. It's natural to have off days. What's crucial is the ability to recognize them and return to your routine.

Stay Inspired:

Regularly Revisit Your 'Why': Remind yourself frequently about why you started this journey. This can rekindle motivation during periods of stagnation.

Seek External Motivation: Read books, watch documentaries, or listen to podcasts that align with your goals. Surrounding yourself with inspirational content can reinforce consistency.

Adapt and Evolve:

Stay Flexible: If something isn't working, be ready to adjust. Consistency doesn't mean rigidity. Adapting to what works for you is crucial.

Continuous Learning: Stay updated with new techniques or tools that can assist you in your journey. Being open to learning ensures that monotony doesn't set in.

Remember, the path to consistency is often non-linear. There will be peaks of high motivation and valleys of reluctance. The key is to stay committed, adapt when needed, and always keep the bigger picture in mind.

Conclusion

As we journey towards the end of this exploration, it's fitting that we begin our conclusion with a moment of reflection. Throughout the pages of this book, we've delved deep into various practices, philosophies, and experiences that revolve around the art and science of self-awareness.

The 'Conclusion' is not just a summation of what has been discussed, but a synthesis of understanding, a moment to distil the essence of all we've learned.

It offers a chance to revisit key takeaways, ponder lingering questions, and project our acquired knowledge into actionable steps for the future.

Let's embark on this final chapter with the same curiosity and openness that has brought us this far, ensuring that the wisdom gleaned from our journey doesn't just end on the last page but becomes a living, breathing part of our daily lives.

Summary of Key Takeaways

The Imperative of Self-Awareness: In a world driven by external stimuli and distractions, the importance of looking inward cannot be overstated. Self-awareness serves as the cornerstone for personal growth, fostering better decision-making, emotional regulation, and genuine interpersonal relationships. Engaging in practices of introspection not only enriches our understanding of ourselves but also transforms our interactions with the world around us.

Diversity of Reflection Techniques: Different cultures have cultivated unique methodologies for self-reflection, showcasing that there is no one-size-fits-all approach. From the meditative practices rooted in Eastern philosophies to the therapeutic models popular in Western cultures, each method offers a distinct pathway to inner exploration.

Reverence of Indigenous Practices: Indigenous techniques emphasize the interconnectedness of the individual with the broader community and environment. Practices such as the Native American sweat lodge ceremonies or the African Ubuntu philosophy highlight the significance of collective self-reflection, where one's identity is deeply intertwined with the community.

Modern Science Meets Ancient Wisdom: Current psychological and therapeutic models, like Neuro-Linguistic Programming (NLP) and Cognitive Behavioral Therapy (CBT), resonate with many teachings from ancient self-reflection techniques. These intersections highlight the timeless nature of human introspection.

Art as a Mirror: Engaging in creative endeavors provides an alternative, non-verbal medium of self-reflection. Whether it's through painting, music, or dance, art allows individuals to express, explore, and understand their innermost feelings, fears, dreams, and desires.

Technological Aids for the Modern Mind: In this digital age, technology offers tools that facilitate self-reflection. Apps, virtual reality, and online courses have made introspective practices accessible to a wider audience, ensuring that everyone, regardless of their background or resources, can embark on a journey of self-discovery.

Customizing Your Path to Reflection: Recognizing that every individual's journey is unique, it's crucial to tailor self-reflective practices according to one's needs, circumstances, and preferences. A mix of techniques, old and new, can provide the most holistic introspective experience.

Commitment to the Journey: Self-reflection is not a one-time endeavor but a continuous journey. The benefits compound over time, making it essential for individuals to remain dedicated, adapting their practices as they evolve.

The Lifelong Journey of Self-Reflection

The pursuit of understanding oneself is an expedition that never truly reaches a final destination. Rather, self-reflection is a lifelong journey, one that unfolds with the meandering path of our experiences, decisions, relationships, and introspections.

It is a deeply personal voyage that often requires navigating the turbulent waters of doubt, confronting the specters of past choices, and charting a course through the unknown terrain of the future.

Self-reflection is not merely a task to be checked off a self-improvement list but a continuous commitment to deepening our understanding of who we are at our core. As we age, we encounter diverse experiences, from heartbreaks to triumphs, stagnation to growth, and everything in between.

Each of these experiences adds layers to our consciousness, prompting us to re-evaluate our beliefs, motivations, and desires. What may have held true for a twenty-year-old might not resonate with the same individual at forty. It is because with each passing year, we're not just accumulating experiences but also evolving in our understanding of ourselves and the world around us.

Moreover, the external world constantly changes, and with it, the societal norms, expectations, and pressures. These external shifts can dramatically influence our internal landscape, often requiring us to reflect upon and adapt our perspectives.

For instance, the challenges and questions faced by previous generations might differ from those of the present, and as such, the process of self-reflection is not a static endeavor but one that morphs with time.

Additionally, this journey often involves wrestling with contradictions within ourselves. We are all a complex tapestry of emotions, aspirations, fears, and talents.

Sometimes, our desires may clash with our values, or our dreams may seem at odds with our current realities. The process of self-reflection helps in untangling these knots, allowing us to align our actions with our authentic selves.

The beauty of this lifelong journey lies not in arriving at a definitive understanding but in the very act of exploring. It's in the quiet moments of contemplation, the sudden epiphanies in the midst of daily life, and the deep conversations that challenge and reshape our beliefs.

Embracing self-reflection means committing to a life where we are perpetually curious, constantly seeking to understand, and forever open to growth.

In essence, the journey of self-reflection is akin to traversing a vast, intricate maze where the destination is not an exit but the myriad paths, turns, and discoveries made along the way.

By understanding that this journey is continuous and ever-evolving, we allow ourselves the grace to change, the patience to learn, and the wisdom to appreciate the profound beauty of self-discovery.

Continue Exploring Self-Awareness

In the vast tapestry of life, self-awareness stands as a golden thread weaving through every experience, emotion, and interaction. Delving into the depths of who you truly are is not merely a journey of intellectual discovery but a profound spiritual and emotional odyssey.

The process of self-exploration is a courageous one, taking one through both the luminous peaks of personal triumphs and the shadowed valleys of doubts and insecurities. And while it may seem challenging at times, the rewards are immeasurable.

Consider self-awareness as your compass, guiding you through life's complexities. The more you cultivate it, the clearer your path becomes, allowing you to navigate challenges with grace, make decisions aligned with your true self, and fully engage with every moment.

Every layer of yourself you uncover adds depth to your understanding, enriching your interactions with others and the world around you. It's an ongoing dialogue between your past, present, and aspirations for the future.

Moreover, the journey of self-awareness is universal, transcending cultural, geographical, and temporal boundaries. Throughout history, countless individuals, philosophers, artists, and everyday people, have embarked on this quest, seeking to understand the essence of their being.

And in their stories, often lie mirrors reflecting our own experiences, challenges, and breakthroughs. By continuing this exploration, you are not only joining this timeless tradition but also contributing to it, with your unique insights and revelations.

The world we inhabit is rapidly evolving, with technological advancements, societal shifts, and personal challenges constantly reshaping our landscape. In this ever-changing milieu, a deep sense of self becomes your anchor. It allows you to remain cantered, irrespective of external turbulence, ensuring you not only adapt but thrive.

Remember, self-awareness isn't a destination but a journey, one that evolves as you grow and change. Each day offers a fresh opportunity to discover a new facet of yourself, to question, to learn, and to connect. And while the path may at times be strewn with obstacles, know that every step, every insight brings you closer to your most authentic self.

So, as you close this chapter and perhaps this book, remember that the true adventure lies ahead. Stay curious, stay open, and most importantly, stay connected to the wondrous, evolving enigma that is you. Your journey has only just begun, and the horizons of self-discovery are endless. Embrace them with an open heart and an eager spirit.

Appendices

Glossary of Terms

Buddhism: An ancient religion and philosophy originating in India, which emphasizes the Four Noble Truths and the Eightfold Path as means to end suffering.

Cognitive Behavioral Therapy (CBT): A psycho-social intervention aimed at improving mental health by identifying and challenging distorted cognitions, behaviors, and emotional responses.

Daoism: A Chinese philosophy and religion emphasizing living in harmony with the Dao, which is a fundamental principle representing the natural order of the universe.

Dreamtime Stories: Indigenous Australian myths that explain the origins and customs of the land, animals, and its people.

Hinduism: A major world religion originating from the Indian subcontinent, encompassing a variety of rituals, beliefs, and traditions.

Journaling: The practice of writing down thoughts, feelings, and observations regularly, aiding in self-reflection and self-awareness.

Mindfulness: A mental state achieved by focusing one's awareness on the present moment, often through meditation.

Neuro-Linguistic Programming (NLP): An approach to communication, personal development, and psychotherapy which posits that there is a connection between neurological processes, language, and behavioral patterns.

Psychotherapy: A general term for treating mental health challenges by talking with a psychologist, psychiatrist, or other mental health provider.

Sweat Lodge: A purification ceremony of the Native Americans, which is a dome-shaped construction intended for spiritual and physical healing sessions.

Ubuntu Philosophy: An African worldview that emphasizes the interconnectedness of all humans, encapsulated in the phrase "I am because we are."

Wu Wei: Translated as "non-doing" or "non-action", it's a Daoist concept that refers to the cultivation of a mental state where actions are performed effortlessly and in alignment with the flow of life.

Virtual Reality Therapy: A type of therapy that uses virtual reality technology to provide immersive experiences for therapeutic purposes, especially effective for phobias and post-traumatic stress disorders.